D1338300

First published 2005 by Walker Books Ltd, 87 Vauxhall Walk, London SE11 5HJ

2   4   6   8   10   9   7   5   3   1

© 2005 Chris Riddell

The right of Chris Riddell to be identified as author/illustrator of this work has been
asserted by him in accordance with the Copyright, Designs and Patents Act 1988

This book has been hand lettered and typeset in Goudy Hundred

Printed in China

All rights reserved. No part of this book may be reproduced, transmitted or stored in
an information retrieval system in any form or by any means, graphic, electronic or mechanical,
including photocopying, taping and recording, without prior written permission from the publisher.

British Library Cataloguing in Publication Data: a catalogue record for this book is available from the British Library

ISBN 1-84428-766-1

www.walkerbooks.co.uk

THE
DA VINCI COD

AND OTHER ILLUSTRATIONS
TO UNWRITTEN BOOKS

WALKER BOOKS

AND SUBSIDIARIES

LONDON · BOSTON · SYDNEY · AUCKLAND

FOR ALL AT
THE LITERARY REVIEW

FOREWORD

There are many shelves in the library of unwritten books, all of them empty. Although this is a drawback for the dedicated reader, it is a positive godsend for the enterprising artist as the number of unwritten books is literally infinite and all of them require illustrations. As the books are unwritten, there are no complicated passages to wade through, no implausible plot twists, no disappointing endings. They take up no space, never get dog-eared, never smell like mouldy underwear, and they are very reasonably priced. But the greatest virtue of unwritten books from the point of view of an illustrator, is that they have no authors - no authors to complain, interfere and pretend they know best. So here, for the first time, collected into a slim volume, fragrantly priced and easy on the eye, are illustrations to some of the finest books never written.

Chris Riddell

TO GRILL A MOCKINGBIRD

THE DA VINCI COD

THE WIZARD OF ODD

Prod and Prejudice

THE IMPORTANCE OF BEING EARLESS

THE SATANIC NURSES

JUDE THE OBVIOUS

ANGLICANISM AND THE ART OF MOTORCYCLE MAINTENANCE

THE LION, THE WITCH AND THE WARDROBE ASSISTANT

2001: A SPACE QUIET-NIGHT-IN

KING SOLOMON'S MOANS

OLIVER BUST

DEAF IN THE AFTERNOON

MANSFIELD PORK

THE PRISONER OF BRENDA

TINY EXPECTATIONS

CAPTAIN CORELLI'S MANDARIN

A WOOLLEN OF NO IMPORTANCE

A ROOM WITH A LOO

THE WITCHES OF EASTBOURNE

TESS OF THE BASKERVILLES

THE WATER ADOLESCENTS

CATCHER IN THE FLY

BLOKE HOUSE

JANE EAR

THE PRIME OF MISS ABERDEEN ANGUS

TENDER IS THE NEWT

A MOUSE FOR MR BISWAS

THE RED BADGER OF COURAGE

THE APES OF WRATH

THE SCREWTAPE LETTUCE

LARGE DORRIT

THE NEW CURIOSITY SHOP

SADDAM BEDE

THE TWEE MUSKETEERS

SPANIEL DERONDA

WUTHERING TIGHTS

THE ACCIDENTAL TORTOISE

THE RAGGED TROUSERED PHILATELISTS

THE DECLINE AND FALL OF THE ROMAN UMPIRE

THE BIG SHEEP

HILDA KARENINA

THREE MEN IN A BOOT

SONS AND PLOVERS

MUDDLEMARCH

THE TENANT OF WILDFELL MALL

BRAVE OLD WORLD

HEART OF DORKNESS

BIG LORD FAUNTLEROY

THE WORLD ACCORDING TO CARP

ALL THE PRETTY DONKEYS

THE SHIPPING MEWS

DAY OF THE TRIFLES

HARD MIMES

THE NOT-SO-CURIOUS INCIDENT OF THE DOG IN THE DAYTIME

VALLEY OF THE TROLLS

NARROW SARGASSO SEA

THE SECRET GORDON

WITH APOLOGIES TO...